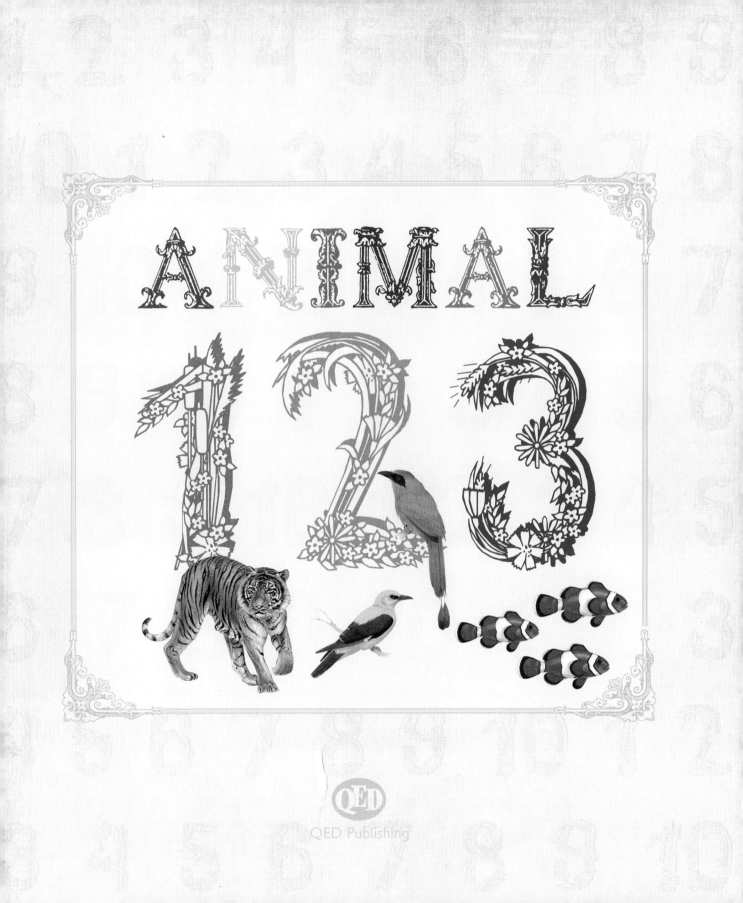

ANIMAL
123

QED Publishing

one

caterpillar

2

two parrots

3

three foxes

four bears

5

five whales

6

six bats

7

seven seals

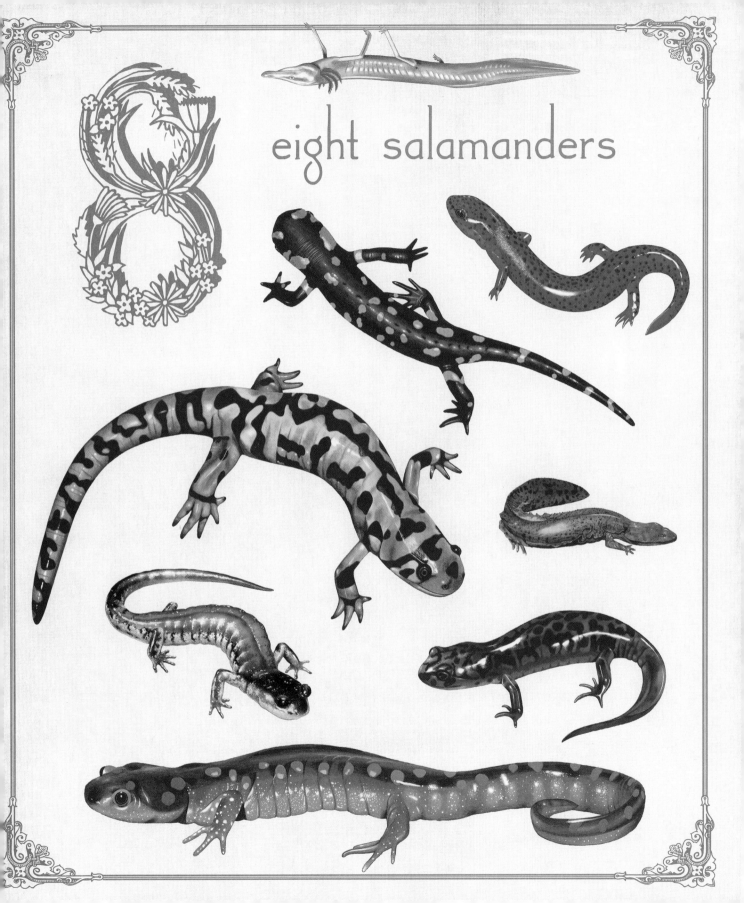

eight salamanders

nine beavers

10

ten spiders

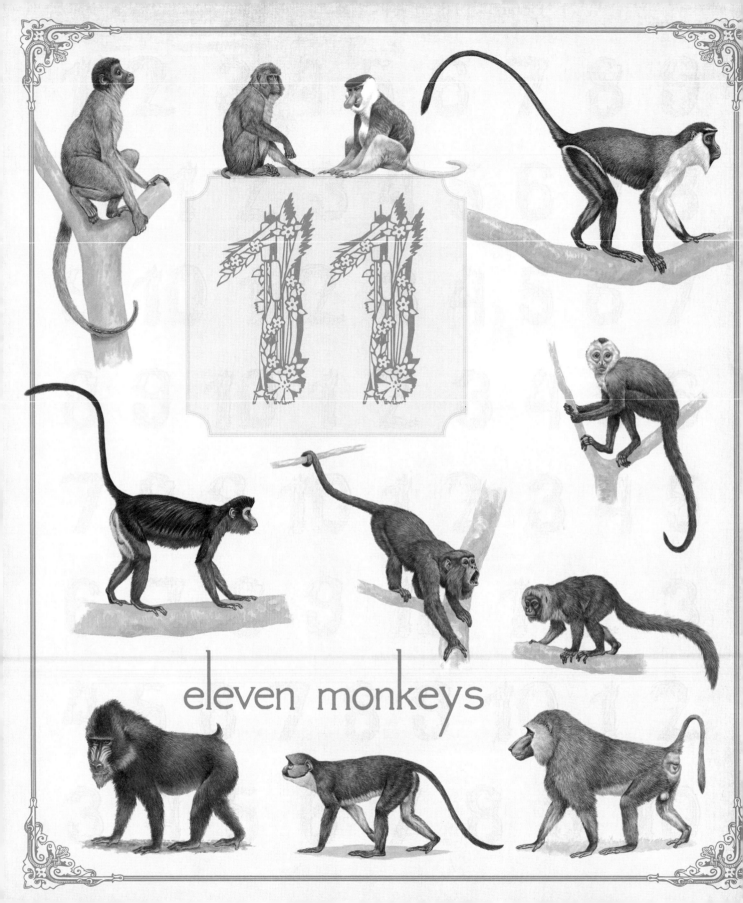

11

eleven monkeys

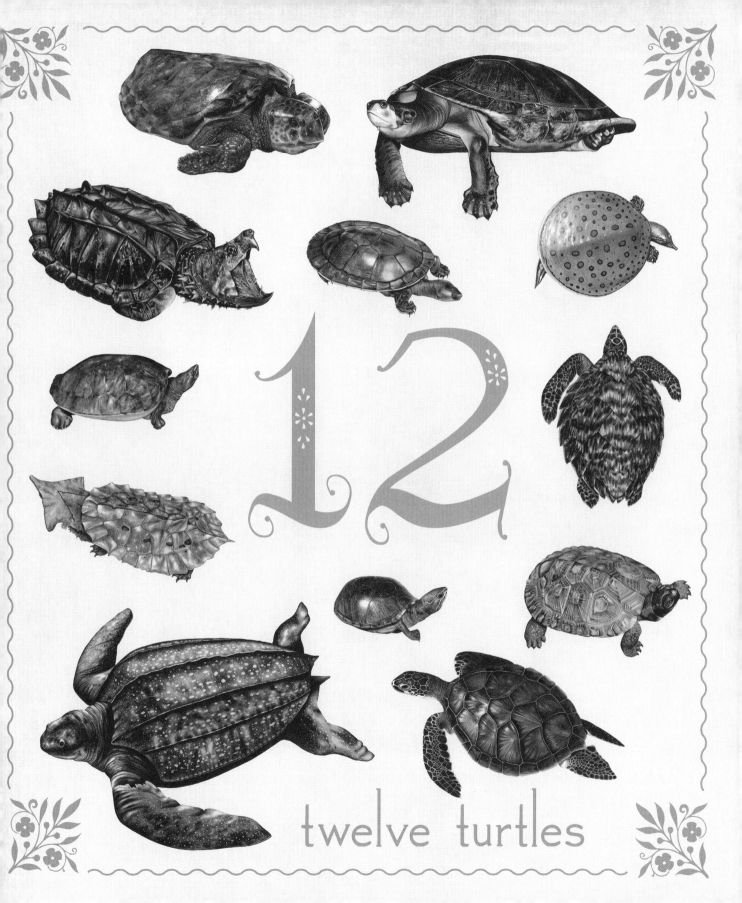

12

twelve turtles

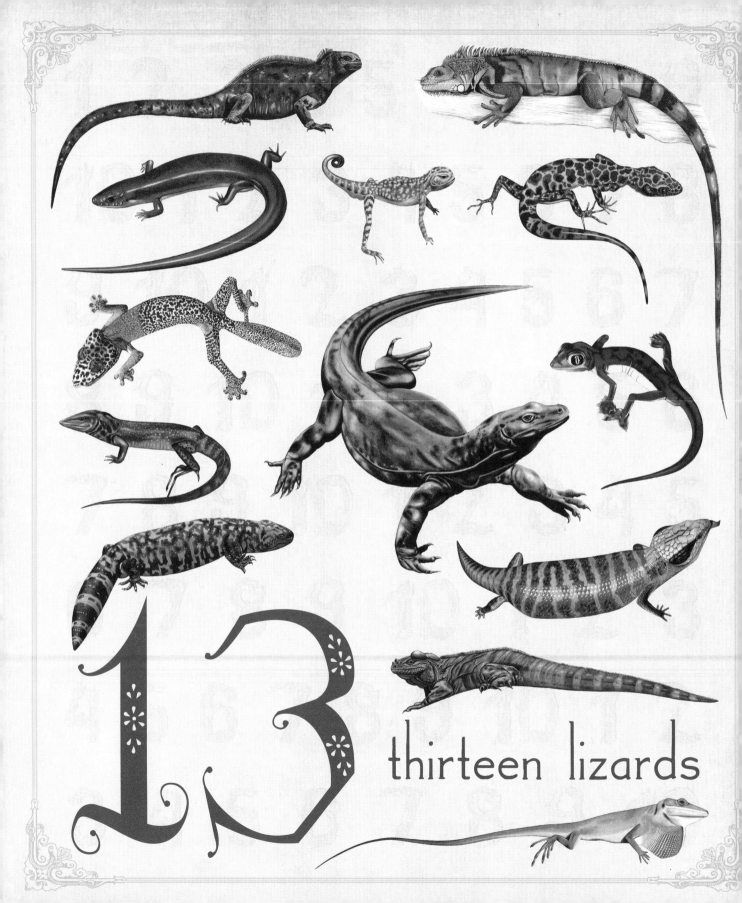

13 thirteen lizards

14

fourteen tigers

fifteen snakes

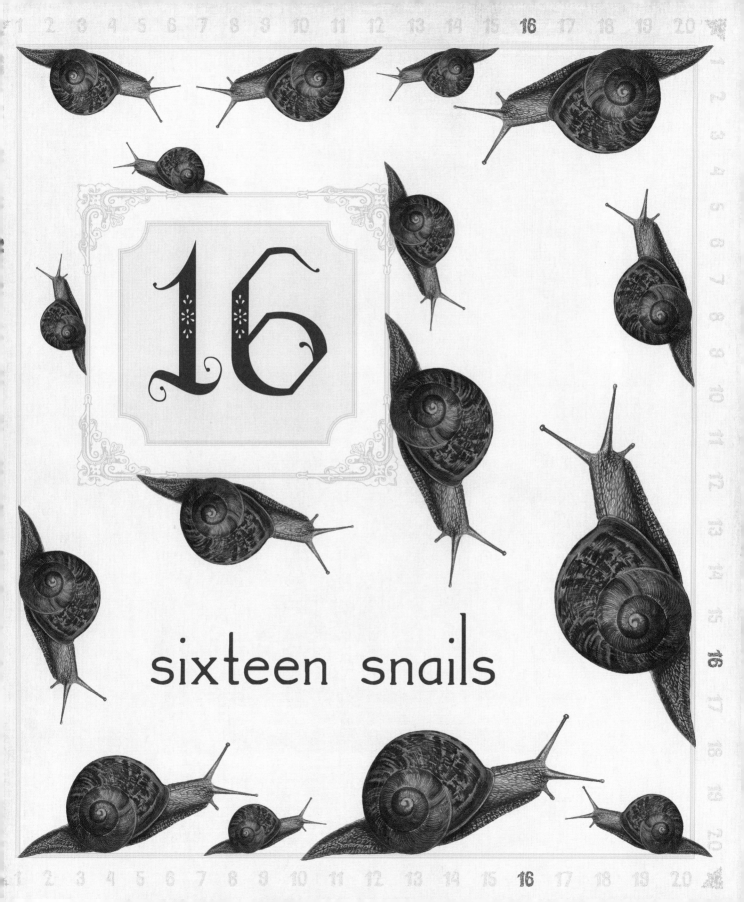

16

sixteen snails

17

seventeen beetles

eighteen birds

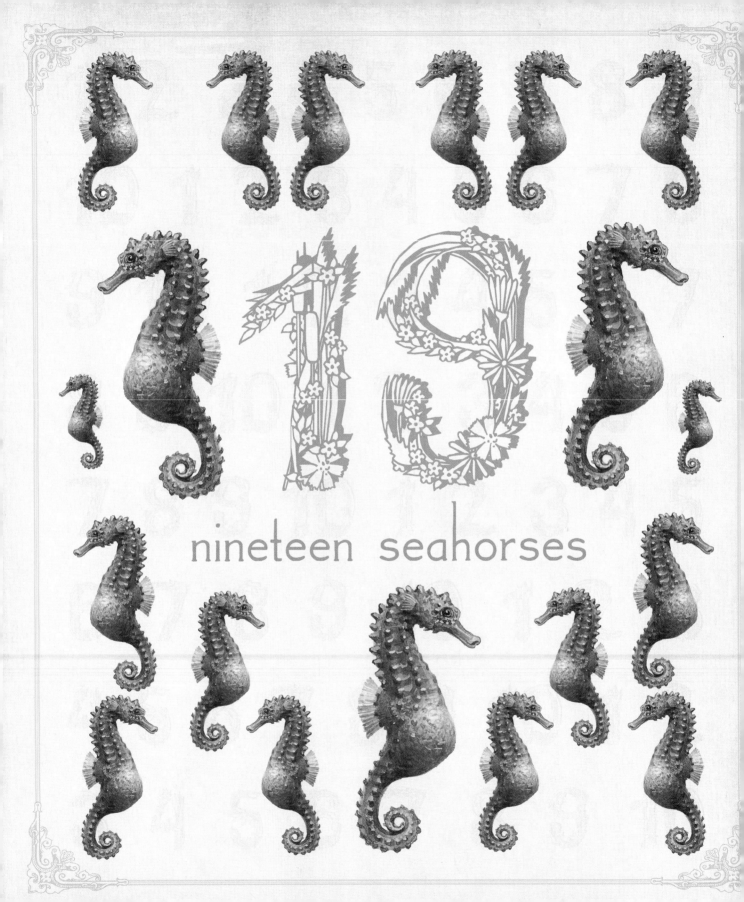

nineteen seahorses

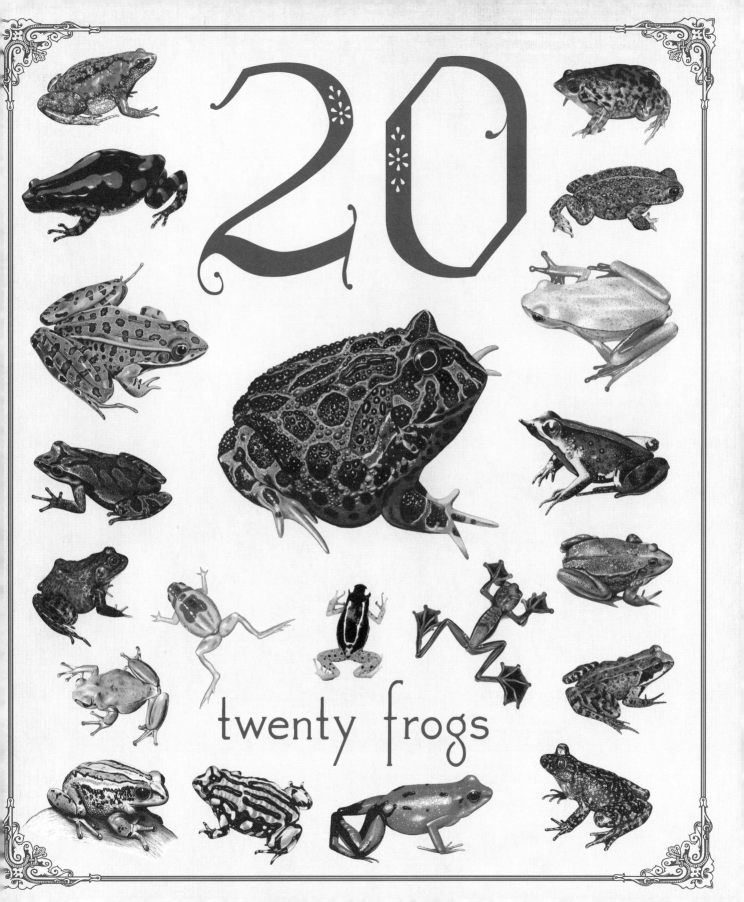

20

twenty frogs

30

thirty flies

forty shrimps

50

fifty butterflies

60

sixty starfish

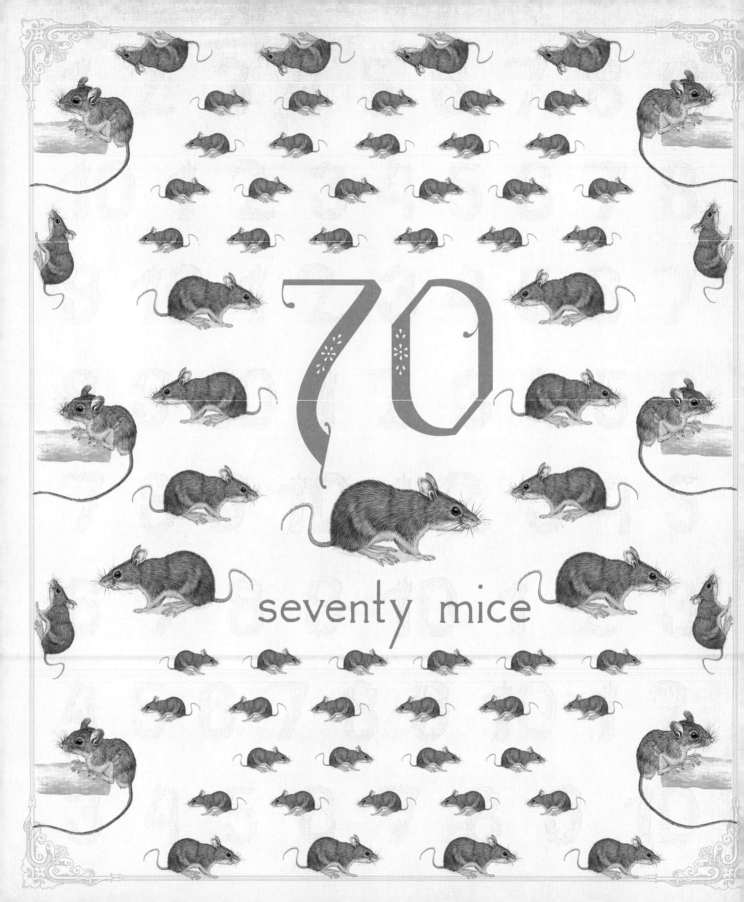

70

seventy mice

80
eighty ladybirds

90

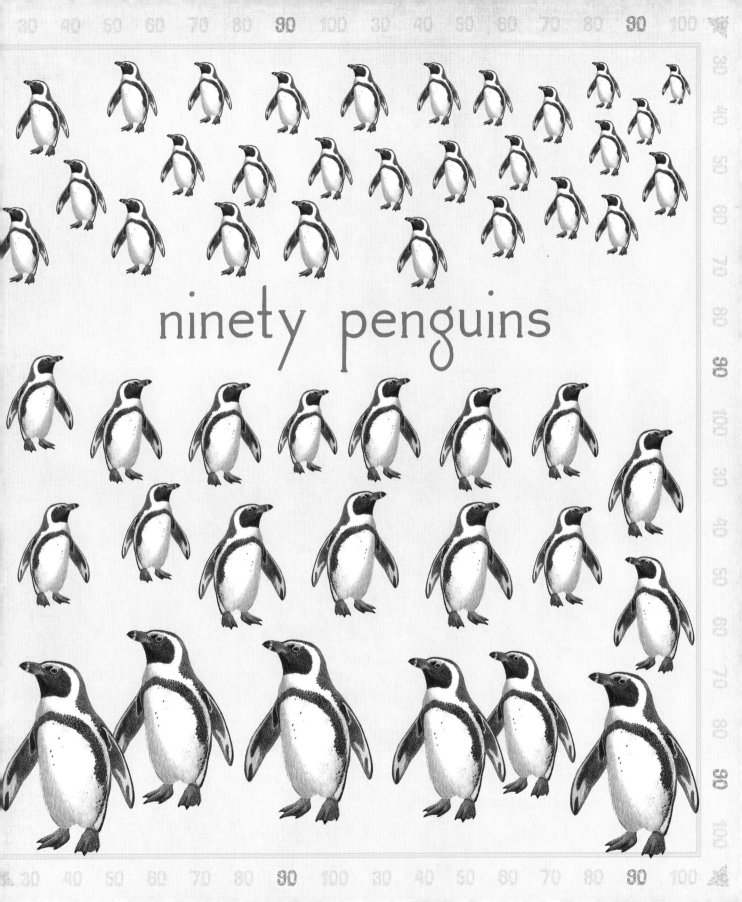

ninety penguins

100
one hundred fish

This edition published in 2014
First published in 2013
Copyright © Marshall Editions 2013

QED Publishing, a Quarto Group company
The Old Brewery
6 Blundell Street
London N7 9BH

www.qed_publishing.co.uk

A catalogue record for this book is available from the British Library.

ISBN 978 1 78171 682 3

Printed and bound in China by
1010 Printing International Ltd

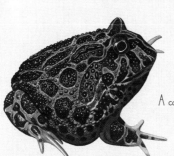